BOOKS BY DAVID BRAZIL

The Ordinary (Compline, 2013)

antisocial patience (Roof, 2015)

The Kenning Anthology of Poets Theater: 1945 – 1985
(edited with Kevin Killian)
(Kenning Editions, 2010)

HOLY GHOST

CITY LIGHTS SPOTLIGHT SERIES NO. 15

DAVID BRAZIL

HOLY

GHOST

CITY LIGHTS

SAN FRANCISCO

CITY LIGHTS SPOTLIGHT
The City Lights Spotlight Series was founded in 2009,
and is edited by Garrett Caples.

Library of Congress Cataloging-in-Publication Data
Names: Brazil, David (Poet).
Title: Holy ghost / David Brazil.
Description: San Francisco : City Lights Books, [2017] | Series: City Lights
spotlight ; no. 15
Identifiers: LCCN 2017000385 | ISBN 9780872867147 (paperback)
Subjects: | BISAC:POETRY / American / General. | POETRY / Inspirational &
Religious.
Classification: LCC PS3602.R399 A6 2017 | DDC 811/.6--dc23
LC record available at https://lccn.loc.gov/2017000385

Cover art © Colter Jacobsen
As the Eagle, the Wild Goose and the Breeze See It (detail)
graphite on record sleeve, 2016

All City Lights Books are distributed to the trade by
Consortium Book Sales and Distribution: www.cbsd.com

For small press poetry titles by this author and others,
visit Small Press Distribution: www.spdbooks.com

City Lights Books are published at the City Lights Bookstore,
261 Columbus Avenue, San Francisco, CA 94133
www.citylights.com

This book is for Carol Estes,
Andrea Davidson and Lynice Pinkard
—mothers in the gospel

ACKNOWLEDGMENTS

Some of these poems have previously appeared. My thanks to the editors and publishers.

"Prayer" appeared in Poems by Sunday; thanks to Daniel Owen and Sarah Anne Wallen.

"To Be Alive While You're Alive," "Nativity Ode" and "Hey Dad" appeared in *Yo, Eos!* (Berkeley Neo-Baroque, 2011); thanks to Chris Daniels.

"Slave Song" was printed as a broadside by Wooden Shoe Press; thanks to Nick Baranowski.

"An Unopened Letter from Diane di Prima" appeared in *A Fiery Flying Roule*; thanks to Eirik Steinhoff.

"Your Leaven" appeared in *Orphica* (Lew Gallery, 2011); thanks to Micah Ballard and Sunnylyn Thibodeaux.

"The Doctrine of the Symbol" appeared in *antisocial patience* (Roof, 2015); thanks to James Sherry and Deborah Thomas.

"The Year That King Obama Died" appeared in *Praxis, Apostles!* (Materials, 2015); thanks to David Grundy and Lisa Jeschke.

Several of the *Holy Ghost* poems previously appeared in chapbooks issued by Compline Press. "Prole Song" appeared in *The Ordinary* (Compline, 2013). My abiding thanks to Michael Cross.

I am so grateful to you all.

"... to decide on the holy ghost ..."

—Ezra Pound

"Is the Holy Ghost any other than an Intellectual Fountain?"

—William Blake

"Light bulb! Holy Ghost!"

—Frank O'Hara

CONTENTS

Prayer 1

Holy Ghost Say 3

To Be Alive While You're Alive 4

Holy Ghost Practice 6

Thirty-Six 7

Holy Ghost Grant 12

One Dust Song 13

Holy Ghost Ask 15

Twa Corbies 16

Holy Ghost Open 19

Kids 20

Holy Ghost Question 22

Tyrant Song (You Know Who You Are) 23

Holy Ghost Channel 25

Prole Song 26

Holy Ghost Channel (II) 27

Diane Arbus 28

Holy Ghost Stand 30

Slave Song 31

Holy Ghost Say (II) 32

The General Strike / The Entry Of Christ Into Oakland 33

Holy Ghost Like 34

An Unopened Letter From Diane Di Prima 35

Holy Ghost Name 36

This Is What The Spirit Bid Me 37

Holy Ghost Joy 41

Essays Upon Epitaphs 42

Holy Ghost Veil 43

To Jane : The Invitation 44

Holy Ghost Veil (II) 45

Sorry I Didn't Notice Your Haircut 46

Holy Ghost Remember 48

O Common 49

Holy Ghost Come 50

A Collect 51

Holy Ghost Face 52

A Coracle 53

Holy Ghost Return 54

What Is Bodhisattva Art? 55

Holy Ghost Rhythm 56

About The Rainbow Body 57

Holy Ghost Tune 60

My Wife, Her Phone 61

Holy Ghost Dawn 63

My Polis 64

Holy Ghost Trace 65

Your Leaven 66

Holy Ghost Go 67

Nativity Ode 68

Holy Ghost Coast 70

Sara's Song 71

Holy Ghost Tone 73

Holy Ghost Go (II) 74

We Serve Lions 75

Holy Ghost Take 79

Infancy II 80

As Mine Commune 81

Holy Ghost Stay 82

For Lacey 83

Holy Ghost Become 84

The Doctrine Of The Symbol 85

Holy Ghost Hear 87

Parousia (The Plaza) 88

Holy Ghost Rime 89

A Wind It Sifts 91

Holy Ghost Play 94

Rime Is The Body Of My Resurrection 95

Holy Ghost Dwell 96

Lylas 97

Holy Ghost Force 99

The Year That King Obama Died 100

Holy Ghost Fold 101

Hey Dad 102

Holy Ghost 104

HOLY GHOST

PRAYER

Prayer for the soul of Karen Dalton
Prayer for the soul of Robert Johnson
Prayer for the soul of Percy Shelley
Prayer for the soul of Charles Olson
Prayer for the soul of Thomas Wyatt
Prayer for the soul of Phyllis Wheatley
Prayer for the soul of Laurence Clarkson
Prayer for the soul of Anacharsis Cloots
Prayer for the soul of Herman Melville
Prayer for the soul of Baruch Spinoza
Prayer for the soul of John Wieners
Prayer for the soul of Louise Michel
Prayer for the soul of Bertolt Brecht
Prayer for the soul of Blind Lemon Jefferson
Prayer for the soul of Marcel Proust
Prayer for the soul of Jack Kerouac
Prayer for the soul of Kurt Cobain
Prayer for the soul of Elliott Smith
Prayer for the soul of June Brazil
Prayer for the soul of Stan Brakhage

Prayer for the soul of John Lennon
Prayer for the soul of Barnett Newman
Prayer for the soul of Frank O'Hara
Prayer for the soul of kari edwards
Prayer for the soul of Stacy Doris
Prayer for the soul of Leslie Scalapino
Prayer for the soul of Dante Aligheri
Prayer for the soul of Christine di Pizan
Prayer for the soul of Billie Holiday
Prayer for the soul of Etta James
Prayer for the soul of Akilah Oliver
Prayer for the soul Shulamith Firestone
Prayer for the soul of Jacques Derrida
Prayer for the soul of Lou Reed
Prayer for your soul & my soul & the souls of everyone
we know and love between us,
prayers for all the liberators and
prayers for those in need of liberation,
we are the same people.
Prayer for the soul of David Brazil.

HOLY GHOST SAY

Say my
name, say my name,
say my name, I
thought I overheard your wishes, we
live in the stutter & from a flaw we gather
butter of the resurrection deliberate as
light after a rainy morning as
instruction. He wed not these
creatures fail to flourish us, but
ripen love within slave gates, the
lord shall be a wall of fire &
there is no veil,
the check good daughter's in the mail.

TO BE ALIVE WHILE YOU'RE ALIVE

To be alive
while you're alive
turns out to be a taller order than
expected, I
get up early for a change & the
moon's still out, with
Venus her consort,
but now it's a little later & that
eastern sun has writ her into
ineligibility,
early morning contrails &
Kensington blues,
smoke or is it steam from the
house across the way,
I wipe condensation off the
big front window with the
flat of hand so I could
see through it, *drosos* is the
word we find in Aeschylus for both

dew & the young of an animal,
xaire Eos,
salve Aurora,
I met dawn just out the
threshold of my dad's house in
forest, Forest Home,
big bird lopes by upon its ground of
wind & the white van's still
parked across the street,
but if Jack Rose,
"Jack, joke, poor potsherd,"
five birds cross, now
visible in distance one last time before
they're vanishing forever forward,
& I was wrong, the moon's
still out, the movement of an
airplane thru the firmament
had drew my eye to it, so
let me attend, let me tend,
"now that I'm a man full grown."
Thanks Dad. Thanks Jack. Thanks, Dawn.

HOLY GHOST PRACTICE

I practice and meditate,
that's all I do.
There are no books about me,
I died, I
died and I live your speaking,
where there are two,
where there is a river of love,
where we tarry with the mystery,
among the memorial stones,
drawing down the consequences,
do you not yet know there aint no grave.

THIRTY-SIX

Thirty six & with the right to
    chant the passage for if I am

lacking in the right at this age when then
    shall I have the chance to

speak my worldly transit in such words as
    you might have my fellow transiter?

Like you I'm the smoke ascending from
    the process in the light that

grows more fierce as day dives
    toward its noon the sun speaks

of a city where we were and built it with
    our loves and sacrifice and how

we weathered seasons lacking info & still
    wandered this is songs that

will not die I'm asking you if you have
    likewise felt this way and

what you did with it, with sun, with
    smoke and human form, to what use then

your most colossal breakfast or these
    words you learned your whole life long,

if not to save at last one human soul or
    thousands by the echoes that

resound in them from logos always working in
    our dormancies, that seizes us in

sleep to reacquaint us every time with
    principles, with aches and with

foundations, so a song a mother sang is in
    your ear two decades hence as

one lost charm of what a love may be when
    you're in need of it, the

sun the smoke the song you frame or utter
all the human city where I found

myself in some way lost but heading for
the clues of any outside to the valley

and a tone shall lead them there,
what's coming through to me through you is

rescue that we get the rope we'll
grab down here so body is

our instrument the doubled heart in it is
what we wake to when we're

tried by fire of the day whose haze is
analog to birth by which we're

set behind a window for to see it, every
lord likes song and mine is heeding

this one as a cause for singing city body our
beloved precinct where I settled

all my loves into the starry crown of Oakland for
    stability in which I've made a pact

so that the heart may sort its portions within
    time to objects that endure there

as the symptom of the vanished underlying
    father we are waiting for

but please dont leave us please dont
    leave us do not render me

an orphan of phenomenon I dreamt your body and
    then you dreamt mine,

the bubble mist or haze or smoke or
    thunderclap of being all this is

does not recuse us from the work of love
    but throws us in it all the more

as we see all the sorrowing in city for what
    calls not for a sorrowing a

cliff I'm living on becomes the vantage out from which I
 see the towers trees and wires all the

houses pickets poles particulars of
 fog which just means elements of

this our common city we agree can
 communicate exchange or

love each other over or else
 mourn and keep on walking or else

tell you what I saw.

HOLY GHOST GRANT

Who dispenses healing from
the folds of hir garment with
is times , the verry syrups yall
cant gather otherwise than incarnation,
tick, the wound, for in still rooms I
had possession, so deaprilled sadde from that
king who had sayde simply : it makes
cords of itself & makes mistakes thereby,
suck tone through a straw &
sit down to lunch, I grant you the
power of binding & loosing, for the
tracklist's lost & it's on to dead
reckoning, son, it just goes on &
on, taking up the same phrase eventually.

ONE DUST SONG

day and dust
and dust and day
and breath and bone
and mortal clay

to say all what
we cannot say
it falls to dust
to dust and day

in god we trust
to show our way
a way to dust
to dust and day

day is short
and dust is long
and right is right
and wrong is wrong

and song is sung
and we shall play
all day long
our dust and day

dust and day
and day and dust
all of what
is living must

say out what
it has to say
before it's dust
while it is day

day and dust
and dust and day
and breath and bone
and mortal clay

HOLY GHOST ASK

Glad in raiment, glad in vestment, glad in the complex kind,
ask after me at the depot, the man there has my number, ask
for the kid made of mud who doth live down the road,
antagonism in the social fabric's just what you expected,
go to work and ask about it there, check out the
pamphlet at the bank, ask your black neighbor is
racism over, or motherfucker just ask me. How
can we keep making art is just another way of saying how
can we live in this world, now answer the question with your
own valiant works and consider your debts to your forebears
in making, you owe them big for everything you are, the
other name for everything you love ; could you
cluster with me by the river named phenomenon and
sing the song that will not die there ? Can you
can you can you ? Take off work, call in sick, call
a strike, shut it down to make a space for that
saint named the lady in red to dance before the
gates of death forever, now in the mind indestructible cold
morning and the righteous action rhetoric cant break.

TWA CORBIES

Two black crows
up in a tree
conversed upon
mortality

The first to the second:
I saw a man
of handsome youth
and with his hand

he waved as though
to comrades dear
but comrades there
were no such near

The second to first:
This selfsame man
has died of thirst
within our land

Without dear friends
or lady fair
he perished and
is lying there

in yonder valley
deep and cold
and noplace is
his story told

and no man knows
that there he lies
alone he lived
alone he dies

The first to the second:
Let us take
ourselves to him
and let us make

our meat of him
who has died there

who was so young
who was so fair

and then they went
unto the youth
those crows whose names
were Wisdom and Truth.

HOLY GHOST OPEN

An obvious tea.
You open your mouth and speak,
  correctamundo,
for sciond, parallels the
        storm one hammer
    for a syntax against death, bust thru
      the walls of sathans house down to the verry foundations &
      fight 'im shoeless if you gotta, did
 you come to see a reed, a
shadow or a mist ? I
      am speaking to move you to shame.

KIDS

And all that we had
settled in our west un

worked itself in drought of
law and famine of the voice

where temple was smeared
blood about the mouth when

word went fatal lacking
grace in gap, so that the

hearts made outside all their
filthied inwards on the mirrors of our

given palaces and they became the
killing grounds of *what we cant work out*

I'm reaching for your hand in the dark I
reach and reach and is it found how

shall I find you in this kid o
where in waste is wisdom hid

HOLY GHOST QUESTION

However I'd communicate with
flowers, with my poverty, or with
this orange glame , the dead. Turn
it out, signal up, the
david gesture builds a rhyme at the caesura.
Of a sudc , in the splendid garden of the lambent forms, I'm
about to ask y'all a question.

TYRANT SONG (YOU KNOW WHO YOU ARE)

We threw down the tyrant wherever he
    came, he came with the sorrowful
face of a friend,

he came in a castle all covered with cypress he
    came with our face & he
stayed till the end

and we in our sadness turned into our
    seeing, the tyrant was us & he
came in our name. He came

with our voices & came with our lovings he
    came with a queen who was at his
right side, he came as in love & he

threw us all down & then grieving to
    do it burned us to the ground.

For all that he gave was a
debt — a debt —
in guise of a gift but
not yet — not yet —
the sorrowful tyrant had
set — had set —
the terms of the dream we
abet — abet —

HOLY GHOST CHANNEL

Splendid world so
passing what's the cincture, what
channel temple in time to set tune,
massaging the vigor of grass but your thousand
shapes of the forgetfulness obsctruct the heart, a
gleaning from it shown up to the altar of rammed earth,
for I became a miror to myself, you the
small man daughter of the eye, according to
my Kronos rule the spirits change their sex like
vowels change a quantity, like birds become real birds

PROLE SONG

chrono
    choked prole
w/ ill dreams
seeks glass architecture,
   sangha, a period
    put to this
epoch of shit.
   Please
communicate direct w/
ground zero at the
   end of time, give
   up races, tear up
your slave money &
   shake hands w/
everyone

HOLY GHOST CHANNEL (II)

You go with the clue cause what
do you got. A table, a work
table covered with blood, the
flesh hooks and scrapers, pro-
minent veins and death in the face, but
Jeshurun kicked, dead a book, a
channel to the heart on order of
a musical phrase, so you marinated in the world & its salt crept,
new new new thing o new new thing

DIANE ARBUS

When I met you on the IRC at work your
    name was *DianeArbus*, all one
    word I dont recall your
real name in the lapse of time we made

a date I guess we were both bored & needed
    fucks or else at
    best some alternation so we met
out at a spot on One Sixteenth the

middle of the day and started
    drinking it was lunchtime I was
    temping at Columbia & didnt give a
fuck the way you can when you are

twenty the whole subway ride was whispering indecencies &
    back at
    your place we were on the mattress for
the thing that I can now recall the least

and afterwards I called my girlfriend from
	your phone the asshole that I was
	in the millennium and some years
subsequent you asked what was she

like I said that she was nice the beer and
	conscience catching up with me and I
	was coming down and no surprise I
never did see you again what was your

name where are you now I wandered once I wandered through
	a city populous a city & I temped a
	ways uptown Columbia I
spent a lot of time at work on line.

HOLY GHOST STAND

Stand foursquare on
love o motherfuckers of
the earth, the
science is to hand for you no picture
saves your sleep neath lassitudes of
lines I cant not say, but this is what is pours
in no topology we know, releasing
bubbles from its baise, conserving
flowers of itself until the fire of all grain resolves the day.

SLAVE SONG

Kingdom weathers
cool and breezy
says that o my
yoke is easy

my tongue's broke on
kingdom speeches
far as Pharaoh's
army reaches

see the song and
sing the slave as
he is laid down
in his grave

then before
astonished eyes
let him within his
people rise

HOLY GHOST SAY (II)

Without eyes, say it, christian son,
    fell down into the plague of heresies, the
    reward of filizl guilt, pile it on dad,
     so what if i never
      fed your graves,
       so far as food
        climb another dunghill kill another pop star
    loiter with nintendo as a participial adulthood,
    just kidding, just kidding, here's a new
    diagram of ethics, it's a lotta work but

THE GENERAL STRIKE / THE ENTRY OF CHRIST INTO OAKLAND

smoke & the
    railed sky, the eth—
ics of the end, con—
trasted by a shar—
    per vigor giving shape to
our get-with-itude when
    we are on top of
    freight in them in—
human spaces of the port, on such walk
alongside friends o—
ver the bridge as the sun sets & we
commence to barf at cops in
    motherfucking choppers, such
long walk with friends that
    we have never taken.
Now I'm so glad that I walked with you & that
    I will have walked.
We stood there in the perfect places, we
    sat down & we ate almonds.
We shut that motherfucker down.

HOLY GHOST LIKE

Blood on the calyx,
blood in the tube,
I'd like to sail in a boat to my wedding, I'd
like to see things clear for once, like
the western city, like justice, like my own
hands. All this normal stuff, you
know, you know the drill, you
had those feelings, you
woke up this morning.

AN UNOPENED LETTER FROM DIANE DI PRIMA

Each one
comes here
to be a worker in it.
Each one comes to work for life.
This place of light we gather is where we will have signed our names
by means of deeds we undertook, were
righteous were unrighteous.
Lord may I find the strength to be righteous.
Lord make my friends strong to be righteous.
Lord defend me from the unrighteous.
Lord defend from their clubs & their poisons,
from them who strike in dark of night,
from them who wound the ones who sleep unarmed.
Lord keep us safe from their armies of death.
My love comes bicycling come.

HOLY GHOST NAME

That you never cease making
the name as a culmination of
all history in wind,
long time and faith you sought the ground,
so try to say,
so try now to say,
what it was you gathered there at
point of most appearance, giving
sense as the gift to our reckonless poverty,
losing letters of the name so that I
wanna know,
I really really wanna know,
how it was o how o how o how it was,
o how o how o how did I get over,
how I got over

THIS IS WHAT THE SPIRIT BID ME

You bid me Spirit tell the force
that brought us to the place of wind
from where our heart ejected by a star
came to the pivot of the restless earth,
the salt of matter we are woven of as
mother of our woes & light yet not to be
disbound from loves of earth are like the

blueprint for the chambers that will answer them,
the earth is full of majesty of god yet
not unlike the sequences of proteins that
coagulate to yield a higher order of the
song still of degrees, for that you did not

know what this word meant until this conversation means
time has another shape and we frail instruments shall
sing it or shall be the singing as such singing

always needs a place, this residue or crust of
light deposited where rivers are then just a

point or phase of cycle we are sundered
from in one part yes but inextricable as
well as breath that always draws you back to

rhythmic unity as freedom within bonds, so liberty or
license then and who says law and
what says grace what says the street which
answers to the day for it's the greenness of
the day whose hidden life we never see,

to settle on a rock and beat it till it yields our food is
education of our spirit by a fire seven times in
this long exodus together yall, and in an endless
night still lit by stars that are the intercessions for

the churches here in town in Oakland or in
Ithaca where someone seized the tower to sound out the
bell when first it fell the leaden curtain of the war

perhaps he was the single sole sane man left in the Union

let those with ears hear what the spirit
says then to the churches, to our unions, to our Omnis, to our
answers, civic dust and animating power such a power

to emplace the plastic things of love we are upon our
little stage to work it out in fire, here where

all we ever loved has been and still we
know we are immortal, our dream houses, our

attentions when they're calmed will yield a
sort of endless quiet ocean at the edge of

things where we had dreamed to set a boat and what
we always lived for was that dreaming,
without which we couldnt even *crave* the

bread, you know? For I have seem them die who
could not eat from failing of the wishing for it,
wishing for to live. And what would be
the good news in the life of such a man.

Good news. Good news. You're going west into
the halcyon where there's a scroll prepared &
all the blanks filled up with every name that
you had earned here & you'll get

to eat up a new alphabet of every resurrected
thing you ever loved there as it was a sort of
town that's founded on a steep raked slope
along the river or some water, say, and
all our gifts we gave here have been knitted there together,
we really did intuit it in wind as world that's
coming just as tenseless coming

and it's coming and then like the wind keeps coming
coming like the wind that fills a sail
    or wind that smoothes our wedding veil

HOLY GHOST JOY

The law is ratified in blood on this
parade ground, every anthem pours like a
libation from the cluster where I found you, not a
nation, gulping down the smoke & this
reiterating sins, but the blister of song grew out of
vowel transforms like a fermentation so
it was not in your power to resist hilaritas, the
joy that comes, the world that comes, ensemble.

ESSAYS UPON EPITAPHS

I am the resurrection and the life

I'll see you on the dark side of the moon

HOLY GHOST VEIL

In my weakness I commemorate thy
passage with adornments, with a
dachshund skin & beryl & with
pavements of sapphire, scattered applause from the
conclave of elders, stranded at a station halfway up,
prepare the veil, glossed breezes for this approbation like
a cliff that gets no rest from sea, like
a natural metaphor to signal the impetuous,
just like tom thumb's blues.

TO JANE : THE INVITATION

Jane it was death that threw open the door
and I'm not saying it was any fun
to be transmitted into more
profounder light as on a plane at dawn

The sun keeps coming and then look it comes
to spell a nonsense of your worldly acts
in light of news of grace whose rumor hums
in every day behind the given facts

It even looks like this here conversation
in a hall that everyone has left;
it even looks like solemn recreation
of the spell we weave to answer death.

If love's the channel death's her other face
for everything we loved death will erase
but even this erasure puts in place
in us the daily strength to run this race.

HOLY GHOST VEIL (II)

Set up a veil, so you can think cloth,
so you can think the wind that rents it,
swaying gently in phenomena as cradle,
all the images of flowers also flowers,
all the friendships friendships,
just as though there never was a war until the evidence,
all tears cured, the rising bell of the song,
a leaflet to your heart on which
the sovran gold of painted saying lays it down again,
all for you this time.

SORRY I DIDN'T NOTICE YOUR HAIRCUT

If you got a haircut I am
    not so good at noticing I
quit shampoo & now I look a
    fright betimes in bathroom mirrors in
which all the prior tenants looked at their
    mortalities in just the way I do, en
route to work & sighing for the
    passage signing on nathless for
one more day of pay to give the
    creditors and maybe buy some nosh to
keep up strength and walk in grace of
    sun although the knees grow weak and if I
was a tenant which I am I would abide there
    humble as a tree that's in some
forest no one ever trod, you feel me, I
    could use an aspirin for this
ache I've got all over like the axes of
    the penalty were all at work in me,

and it could shine and birds could ride to
    settle in this measure, cleanly, not without

regard for all this history that had to heap so
    I could reach the fruit of law, this
shellmound has been here six thousand years & I,
    I am the creature of a day, I
look into the mirror I'm en route to work &
    then you blink & it's the tenant that's to
follow, heaving up two flights of stairs her goods
    of this world & then sighing in her ownership.

We made this grave together and we dance in it, that's if
    we're not too shot from work, and if our
knees hold out, and if our teeth don't
    shatter on the shells of law, and if
today's a sun and calm with which
    we maybe make professions.
Underneath the cloud I saw the sovran tree
    that fed the peoples of that town sufficient
for their nutriment no mast who comes for
    this tree's leaves were for to heal the
nations and we ate them in the time of

healing and my children feel it in your bones.

HOLY GHOST REMEMBER

And in how remember this
dwelling, and to render it
according to its pattern, still the petition caesura
doesnt delete, go long, go real long, to the
land without law, and get thyself a wife and flock there,
fuck with me and see what happens,
I'm the grave of all demotic speech,
that from which the hierophant comes forth in
bulletproof vestments befitting occasion, destructio of
templum as the thing cut off, for cash will do,
will do, just cash, just cash, this
is the tomb of the fall of jerusalem which is
two places, which one's which, for
what do you pray.

O COMMON

O common
o barren
o head of the sister

o common
the heart now
of any resister

o justice
the body
of each reinsister

o holy
the visage
of each one who kissed her

HOLY GHOST COME

Then come the thunder of opening strains,
teleport to the heart all judgment, fix the
pinion that communicates to thence, far thrown, the
truth as we may grasp it, for what is just done here founds
justice or opens its door, past
measure the suppliant.

Arising out of war the song we strain to hear.

The body of such saints truth's synonym,
therefore am I edified as all get out.

A COLLECT

O song how shall I pay the rent
O sun how shall I eat
And shall I get back what I spent
On whiles and winds and wheat

O bird how shall I pay the tithe
O day what shall I sell
To have enough to feed myself
And some for you as well

O friend show me another law
Than cash the king of all
And I shall go to service there
When I have heard the call.

HOLY GHOST FACE

I have the veil, I have
this human face, a job,
consistency and flowers,
smoke, the bits of lore, a
view, a little cradle of the law,
some chances, some green
plants, some light by which to work,
an asking price, a secret life, a
soul, any destiny in theory but
the cadences are mine,
you write the same things down again,
you go through your life singing o the same song,
but listen for the changes, breaks, elisions,
reemergence of the theme, the
limbs of the song you have gathered from the face,
that mediate infinite mode.

A CORACLE

As I am a coracle of grace
      in place
I'll make the law to give me just a chance
      to dance,
I'll ask the wage to give me just a break
      to take
Myself and all my partners to the beach
      so each
Can bathe themselves in currents of the sea
      as we
are those who have a need to be so laved
      and saved
For seasalt washes out the ancient blood,
      its flood
Has virtue in itself to make our soul
      grow whole.
The sea itself will wash our mortal part,
      and heart.
And if you want to come I'll see you there.
      Take care.

HOLY GHOST RETURN

You know how return works like
music, like the war. There
is an image and we have to destroy it. Time's
the gift that honors this sword, by means of which
we have the measure that can comb it out. I'll say
that every woman born in Oakland, born in
Zion has subsumed us in the record of this choice,
so that among the firstborn of the dead there is raised one,
the shadows of these genders shall not touch him,
the wounds of any polity unscathe him, com-
ing from the Cloud like any stranger give him welcome, sell
blood as needful, for these is but one thing needful, that's
to heed it, all you list hath lived in your flesh & rights
are not the concept, rather just that light in-
create light that
always has the force to spur remembrance.

WHAT IS BODHISATTVA ART?

compassion

amendment

dedication of merit &

temporal radiance

(open to temporal radiance)

THE ABIGAIL HOTEL

HOLY GHOST RHYTHM

Founded on love's throne we enter the storm.
The left hand is of gold, gold is
this world's figure of rhythm scratched out of hives,
for rhythm is justified of children. Let
the despot run his coronation in this wise, it is
the hand of cruelty, to be expelled in the fulness.
Over our head the devouring flower of transit, which
we forget, which we neglect, we
had to go to work. Apology's beside the point.
The right is Sehkmet, holding nothing, opposite of
life you stood before with loves and prepared places,
where you grew up, those reflections, are the
very blue cloth of this day, the cloth you're
vouchsafed, one emblem of friendship, for if
we are friends then I shall shelter you, there
fore come into rhythm, o my heart, I
live in your transit, in the prevalation of
this portal that has opened by degrees.

ABOUT THE RAINBOW BODY

the teacher said : how old are you ?
the student said : I'm seventeen.
the teacher said : is it your body or your nature that is seventeen ?
the student said : is it your hair or your mind that is white ?
the teacher said : my hair is white, but not my mind
the student said : my body is seventeen, not my nature

If you fail to take the rainbow body you may return as
    soldiers in Afghanistan.
If you fail to take the rainbow body you may return as
    presents vomiting fire in the midst of
    vulgar soliloquoys to justice.
If you fail to take the rainbow body you may
    return as one judging, *oligopistoi,*
If you fail you may return as
    little Eichmanns trying to get paid,
If you fail to gain the rainbow body you may find
    yourself a hungry ghost whose
    wishes have no bottom, like the drunkard who
    would drink the sea & still be without satisfaction,

like a sieve that pours out all the water,
like a man who looks upon his natural image in
a glass and then walks away forgetting then what
    kind of man he was,
If you fail to gain the rainbow body you may become
    a cop blockading Gill Tract,
defending property against need, quite an action to be
    spending your human life doing,
for what is present's also of the judgment,
whatever is a person's share goes into the body of light,
behold I show you a mystery,
giving protection includes helping those oppressed by
    despotic rulers, governments or criminals,
for earth's body turns to heaven's body,
rot to luminescence,
shame to grace,
waste to power, '
mind to spirit,
the living to the soul-founding,
the dust to the sky,
the wasteable to that which can not waste,
the brosial into the ambrosial,

heavenly sweetness of the righteous acts on earth so
   do your best to get it right I—

   Ris is waiting to clothe you in the
   raiments of your holy lineage.

HOLY GHOST TUNE

Any bit of tune will do
to work this work of opening the heart,
for tune is tone that reaches back into the flesh of loves, a
posy writ upon the
cross stretched out like time, like
mind in time, dis-
tended and restlessly seeking to
lay it in figures, what without relent
expands past any figure & then rhymes w/ self as it so does, this here
line and this here break, coordinate in distances, could
feed you for a moment by the law they seem, a-
tremble in the wind, like us before the judgment, this
catena's stitched from just such moments, motes
of the instantiated justice.

MY WIFE, HER PHONE

My wife she slept
as in a frieze

and dreamt a dream
she could not seize

and there beneath
her cover lay

in still and peace
for just this day

and in that room
we called our own

came slight sonatas
from the phone

a phone that told us
time of day

a phone that set us
on our way

a phone that told us
what we know

a phone that told us
where to go

and my wife slept
and I stayed up

to figure how
to fill the cup

of blessing that's
been given me

which is the ceaseless
work to see

HOLY GHOST DAWN

For from the father's house I bore these
splintered pieties and cloth,
neglecting all his instruments of measurement and
balladry and walking out forever into dawn, like
the dawn of this here day. If there were Virginia.
If there were an army I would field it. You
venture up real fast into a light that shines like fire.
This world's an arrest to
prepare you to see.

MY POLIS

my polis is a
gnostic
happenstance

meaning, after I write the above, I
get a letter re:
"the polis,"

(Jason Morris),

quoting back to me   "the
field is us"

HOLY GHOST TRACE

For circumambient to him is
this flame's girdle like a
skirt communicant devouring the
mountain of my passing world, pre-
serving only what is anchored in
the rolling tone of telling how it was, and
known to us as strata of the
read-out names which saved into their fate as
                        spirit's music
bump from out the earthly radio by
accident that's graved to trace,
as permanent as god.

YOUR LEAVEN

make your leaven not
of shit &
wounds
but out of salt,
for son thou art

HOLY GHOST GO

A little barb from the beaches of home,
be glad as you tread from the wastes into refulgences of
song as a clearing whose light's residuary legatee of
having walked whichever here as part of this impassible surplus we
    dont
map in the breeze, for how long have we stalked the bord of
this deleted quarter, asking asking asking asking, then the
cloud and dwelling in the cloud, then the holy table where we offer,
then so many winds which animate our neighbors into these long
    lines,
for hourly we're set to grieve and have a cause to grieve, but
no man's born a christian and you aint born singing either,
go down weeping with a bag full of seeds,
come home laughing your arms fulla sheaves.

NATIVITY ODE

the saintly Vail of maiden white, the
sky a solid wall of cloud like
armies massed against our vision,
which obstruction wrecks how
we would live among each other &
within, I can see individual drops of
the storm that is coming, not a metaphor or else
itself but a metaphor also, & we
find ourself a stray in that abyss of
figuration, by which one's made what, an
intercessor among men, *the*
Greek alphabet was the real trojan horse,
you study all your life to make some
bare conclusions via which you maybe
shrive yourself, it's
nothing fancy after all, a *bare*
common, a roadway, this morning, some
little ditty no overhearer would
understand as prayer, we offer to
whichever second person might be

auditing our plight, *gay*
transports soon end,
for if such Holy Song
enwrap our fancy long,
we give to them what our hands got
pure enough to hold without burning,
false priest that I am,
& this the warning song, *there,*
Would that all God's people were prophets,
and the christmas morning storm stars up.
A cough, Charpentier, a little white in
bottom center "like a rushlight," go's
in the imperative, "*GO !*"
And these three things alone remain,
rattling around the bottom of my backpack.

HOLY GHOST COAST

Where'd we
get these jams, the
junkhouse ma, an
aspiration in the civil conflict finding
tone where it starved in a field, to
fat it up until there is a league of us most
just to tension within stuff, or say do
seeds of wars find soils in your houses, yes or
no, I travelled up the coast to ask, ghost
coast, ghost me, ghost you, the
only residue of us is how you answered.

SARA'S SONG

flesh is grass
my lass
my lass

we who walk
and we who pass

fol de rol
my soul
my soul

meet my man
and pay my toll

toll the bell
oh well
oh well

sell off what
you have to sell

answer love
my dove
my dove

show me what
you are made of

HOLY GHOST TONE

All those easts I dreamt in tone came west, to where
the thunders of the province lent a restless echo,
so I'd fast & sulk in the waste places, while the
sovrans made their entrances into the settlements.
It was I who said there Ð wars were a mouth of blood,
as though the people didnt know, as though the war were not the
    fount
of all our instruments and means. Talk, talk, it will be
marked against you, it'll bubble through the swale, my dearest
chalk marks, o my accidents, my grieving pals. I'm just as much
beneath the sun & looking for the line but *to resist the figure*'s still
the going task, among them to rejuvenate the coronation odes
    from, like
inside, so their *berceuse* of pit becomes our drinking song when we
gulp honey mixed with threads of blood of those who have
    possessed us how
ever it came, our feet washed twice and we at table with the
liberated animals and neighbors, you and me and god, the salt at
    last.

HOLY GHOST GO (II)

I woke up where
I didnt know
before I knew
it was time to go

WE SERVE LIONS

We serve lions, cut
the paths to
myth of heavens eye,

so stress of each was
audience as
we appeared to try

the tree or mother of
the road or letter out
of which

we're said was only
just an organ of
the tempered stitch

that ordered us to
power from the
holy head whose spring

or eye whose
fulness was the space in
which was seen no thing

of city come to
pass so we for
whom the light is sown

could take the
sleep that murders us
and claim it as our own

and musing on the
government of
heaven that we saw

whence traveled soul in
to this strand as
interdict of law

so much that the
dark cortege that
spreads its poison hid

will go to any
length to stamp out
what the righteous did

a channel opens in the
grave of
matter for the skin

that's balanced against
pulses & the
nothing that's within

the legions who have
undecided
all alongside come

to find at final
tally they're
the zero in the sum

and we serve lions we
are towns of
mothers of the made

whose consequence is
catalyst & each word
cannonade

and every sort of
weapon's coruscating from
our care

whose palace has
a priceless blessing
sons & daughters there

and sleeping sleep of
fate at last for
every cloven meter

so that we might in
our own time find
flesh to be repeater

HOLY GHOST TAKE

There was a job to do in
America, communicant with
suffering of the father so
high in a rented bathroom, next
the shades, with infinite griefs of the
human heart laid amongst its befallments,
my father plaied,
my father, his
instruments inoperative like
schedules of sacrifices in the
house of death, go to
that infinite night, go
back, the body transduces all
woes to remind us, & your
real is this parcel so
narrow but
communicant, you
take a tiny number   of them out
of this life in your hand,
the hand that's dreamed out of your earthly hand.
The earthly liturgy.

INFANCY II

New thing, fare
well to unjust blood, a
short walk to alpha &
forsaken shield, an
other sunny day the / /
seeming endless gardens,
welcomes, thanks, phones,
thanks, a sinister twitch as
sex is gratefully purged,
we grow rich in remembrance having
shucked it the fuck off forever.

AS MINE COMMUNE

as mine commune
represents
to seek the routes &
set the rents

we scale the sky come
trimming time and
read the seed to
check the rime

HOLY GHOST STAY

If you make a frame the wind.
If those befallments are your transit take it. The
story isnt worth it for its own sake dont forsake it. There
has to be material to tremble. This
is if you wish to go communicant.
For grace must go its route &   the
fat heart stunts. What
happened is real, dont
turn, how can I
play crying, my
last request is you
play at my funeral, say
*re*creation right. It
goes, we stay.

FOR LACEY

This unstained body given up for life
like dirty shirts or six tons of the law
at some remove resolves into analogies like
tympana whose figures show
the graven rigors of the dispersed judgment
in which one crumb of goodness sifted out
will save you like a
seed of light to build the
holy tree forgetful Eve we
walk down Telegraph and say
these very bodies and we're
laughing at the leap a
waits us Lacey they'll
ordain you who am I to judge.

HOLY GHOST BECOME

Infinite debts to the
brothers through glass. For
if you know all that I
know we are friends.

Do you know the
laws of the passage, can I
ask you some questions?

For I cant be
what I must become lacking
you.

THE DOCTRINE OF THE SYMBOL

The symbol comes to us out of the mouths of the death.
It is the work of those in the grave to weave it.
This is like Penelope waiting for Odysseus.
He is always of course going to come home.
This is narrative.
We'd be disappointed otherwise.
In the same way we will always be going to find the dead.
We'll be the youngest in their number, some day soon.
So the symbol is a sort of echo.
Echo loved us but could only say the last part back.
When the dead find something in us to resonate off of,
that's how they do this work.
This is the original theory of music, as a science of
    the passions.
Of our bondage to the passage.
The dead are fortunate because they're quieted, though
    often very
bored out there in orbit round the moon.
Anything got by us in this trough is an attempt at metrical help.
There's no doubt but that the bond of flesh has made

us obstinate.

But having sifted up from the woe a grain of remembrance,

temples can be made in any place, to

aid us through the strait.

I'm not the first one to have noticed this,

but you have to look hard amidst all the rubbishes.

HOLY GHOST HEAR

We hear so much of death,
we rarely hear of immortality.

       say
     amÐtam

   say:
   these are prepaid tickets,
   we got to be back.

PAROUSIA (THE PLAZA)

And then when on the plaza with the people,
    plaza's just a place & we
    all die, where present inter

change with past will rupture us like
    pavement stones I
    stood in sun & wind & fold & you

did too, elected by the flow to be seen by
    the woven history of us as net in
    side the war deducing love from over

flow which ran in to our beards and over all
    our dirty clothes & wishes & the
    roots in stone, this

city where we came and into which we
    keep on coming cause we're here I
    put my hand up to your heart to

HOLY GHOST RIME

Enameled pairs
from out the tea box,

dragons, locusts,
lions, doves,

the lion of
evangelist the

eye the void the
peacock will all rime

with women and the
cote &

runes that you cant read

say I am so glad I found you in this
    war no death will turn me from the
    love of you this joy I have the

world this joy I have the world where
    for a time the song was heard &
    we stood on the pavement learning words

and healing wounds that rose the very wounds which
    in the holy memory shall be the
    signs and banners even now

A WIND

A wind it sifts the pages of my book
to seek just what it was that I had took
from each day it was given me to look —
on wind that sifted pages of my book

to show them either blank or they attest
to all of what was worst and what was bnest
to all of what I cursed and what I blessed
and what was blank or what I did attest.

For where o pilgrim is our kingdom built
when all our precious labor's stained with guilt
and all our precious gathered milk is spilt
then where on earth's our coming kingdom built

the kingdom comes and then it keeps on coming
through all the daily doldrums that keep numbing
through roaring and all grieving and the humming
kingdom comes and then it keeps on coming

onward soldiers any faith
for while you have a snatch of breath
right then your love's as strong as death
so onward soldiers any faith

and this our standard this our song
through the valleys of all wrong
that we are singing all night long
this our standard this our song

that I will love my enemy
and pray for her most fervently
and work to set her spirit free
and I will love my enemy

and I will be the worldly peace
that's paid for by my own disgrace
and bloodied be my human face
but I will be the worldly peace

and show the world my lord's high law
in what I learned and what I saw

that any given heart might thaw
at last before my lord's high law

that says we shall not make a name
by building towers for such fame
as we should thereby strive to claim
from having made ourselves a name

and arrogantly saying all
who hear should answer to our call
and joining join us in the fall
of we who sought to build the all

such debts shall never be repaid
except by him who is the head
and of whom it is truly said
that he must lead and we be led

the seed to rise must first be sown
where on the earth it dies alone
unrecognized unblest unkown
and having no body now but your own

HOLY GHOST PLAY

The dead are thirsty rather than hungry;
water and wine are poured on their graves.

I dont know where the
song is going to go.

    I'm gonna be vibrating that
    whole plastic ceiling off.

    I'm gonna play till I get
      one sound.

    That I was born for,
      so to speak.

RIME IS THE BODY OF MY RESURRECTION

Rime is the body of my resurrection
made apostolic in portals from here
so that the after will yield a correction
to each mortal garment and each earthly fear

When time is the instrument grace is the measure
for each passing lineament mercy cant hold
and when o my love shall we have the leisure
to see how each would that we are might unfold.

We bring them forth out of our sovereign appointments
with hours that shine in the mornings like stars
and then like the oil of priestly anointments
point up just where in the circuit we are.

I answer blessings outside of a prose,
for we are not on earth as you suppose.

HOLY GHOST DWELL

We also dwell in intervals that
follow transits, I am
speaking to you out of such right now, the
apostolic crisis of
getting up in the morning to
say what you saw & to
see the things that are in
light of that light,
for which the law we
ever after need a veil, I
deal directly, would
Massachusetts ever after give me their
addresses please, a
plantation &
what do you grow, to
narrow it down for
    verily evry distraction's a
foretaste of hell, the
bright, for then came winter to
hotblooded men.

LILAS

It's written here but it will travel,
    nourishing a soul in passage thicker
        by its love & routed

homeward, in the wind like ships like
    word itself a dirge but we with
        open ears sublunary

will listen for it here as echoes of
    celestial loves, so may we
        grow back from the

flood, so fed by fat of earthly water figured
    in the cup to turn a
        spirit of the word in

heart, a ladder, song, for I am but a
    phrase of earth said rain, one
        thousand tears of all our

yields are gathered up and mixed and drunk to
    make a piece of newer day,
        from which is seen

what lives within the double song, or what
    I did not see, the
        mystic cypher shown

to those who read our days in texts alone,
    and this as just a poem but yet
        fused the once with

heat and stillness and the cry of birds and
    mortal hearts still heaping blood of
        law to

make it pure so we may pass on what
    was given us and have it
        be of use,

of use to you who you may be.

And how hard we fought just to
    love you like sisters.

HOLY GHOST FORCE

When I say ghosts.

I mean the healing force of the universe.

To see for myself what they suffer.

I lost my face altogether.

I took on the face of my brother.

Coming out to build that heart.

THE YEAR THAT KING OBAMA DIED

And then we came to Rome it was
the year that king Obama died you
came as far as taverns out to meet me saying
Holy Holy Holy so to tell the doctrine we have
heard it said that I said that to see they will not
hear o vipers I who lived within a people coming nigh to
Rome that hear but do not understand my
intertext that chimes throughout the law o
mercy on my guilty heart in this my rented room but
burn it out like vipers in a furnace by your justice so that
those who sought the Life are pledged by fire's yielding to them I
a man of unclean heart has come as far to beg that in this
way thy mercy's shown to make it fall upon you for we
shant be props unto ourselves I said how long O
Lord I said how long till we repopulate Detroit, our
hearts, the holy seed for which this land, our hearts, how
long O Lord, for we are resurrection people.

HOLY GHOST FOLD

You are living
even now in
ancestors of
future dances.

My son we pass
my son we fold
consider the objects
brought to the table.

Out of what is
can you see those shapes,
how keen is your heart
how sharp is your ear.

HEY DAD

Hey dad, this is
David writing you from
the land of the living,
sun shining the traffic
passing & Coltrane playing
"Greensleves" in my living
room, for real, how's
the weather there, is it
as boring as you thought it was
gonna be, is there anybody there ?
Here there's wind in the
limbs of the plants Sara put
on our fire escape for the light,
for light is sweet,
I've been running fevers but I'm trudging
through the wall of clouds this
incarnation is, I've got friends & projects,
steady work for now,
I'm reading lots of bios to figure out
what kinda man it's possible to be,

what kinda *person*,
just cause you're not the absolute of my
horizon doesnt mean that I don't love you,
dad,
it's just that I'm a singularity myself,
and by the way I live in California now,
why didnt you ever move to a nicer climate ?

A lot of your books live in my house now.
You taught me some apotropes.
A white bird flies by followed by a black one.
I'm going to write a book about you and this is
going to be the last thing in it.
But the last thing always echoes, dont it,
like the clatter of this typewriter, and
meantime picture me here, out far past where you are, I'm
stirring the porridge,
just like you said.

HOLY GHOST

"What is me gonna *do* ?"

CITY LIGHTS SPOTLIGHT

1
Norma Cole, *Where Shadows Will:*
Selected Poems 1988-2008

2
Anselm Berrigan, *Free Cell*

3
Andrew Joron, *Trance Archive:*
New and Selected Poems

4
Cedar Sigo, *Stranger in Town*

5
Will Alexander, *Compression & Purity*

6
Micah Ballard, *Waifs and Strays*

7
Julian Talamantez Brolaski, *Advice for Lovers*

8

Catherine Wagner, *Nervous Device*

9

Lisa Jarnot, *Joie de Vivre: Selected Poems 1992-2012*

10

Alli Warren, *Here Come the Warm Jets*

11

Eric Baus, *The Tranquilized Tongue*

12

John Coletti, *Deep Code*

13

Elaine Kahn, *Women in Public*

14

Julien Poirier, *Out of Print*

15

David Brazil, *Holy Ghost*

16

Barbara Jane Reyes, *Invocation to Daughters*